STARS OF SPORT

MICHELLE KWAN

BY RAYMOND H. MILLER

KIDHAVEN PRESS™

THOMSON
™
GALE

San Diego • Detroit • New York • San Francisco • Cleveland
New Haven, Conn. • Waterville, Maine • London • Munich

© 2003 by KidHaven Press. KidHaven Press is an imprint of The Gale Group, Inc., a division of Thomson Learning, Inc.

KidHaven™ and Thomson Learning™ are trademarks used herein under license.

For more information, contact
KidHaven Press
27500 Drake Rd.
Farmington Hills, MI 48331-3535
Or you can visit our Internet site at http://www.gale.com

LIBRARY OF CONGRESS CATALOGING-IN-PUBLICATION DATA

Miller, Raymond H., 1967—
  Michelle Kwan / by Raymond H. Miller.
    p. cm.—(Stars of sport)
Summary: Discusses the personal life and figure skating career of the young Chinese American who has won numerous awards at the U.S. Nationals, World Championships, and the Olympics.
Includes bibliographical references and index.
  ISBN 0-7377-1540-5 (hardback : alk. paper)
1. Kwan, Michelle, 1980—Juvenile literature. 2. Skaters—United States—Biography—Juvenile literature. 3. Women skaters—United States—Biography—Juvenile literature. [1. Kwan, Michelle, 1980– 2. Ice skaters. 3. Chinese Americans—Biography. 4. Women—Biography.] I. Title. II. Series.
  GV850 .K93 M55 2003
  796.91'2'092—dc21

                                              2002012557

Printed in the United States of America

Contents

America's Skating Sensation

Michelle Kwan practically grew up on the ice. She started taking lessons in the sport of figure skating when she was five years old and won her first competition at age seven. After years of hard work and dedication, including moving far from home to train, she became a world-class figure skater in the mid-1990s. She combined the perfect blend of athleticism and grace in her programs, and she became a crowd favorite. She won the first of her six U.S. Figure Skating Championships (also called Nationals) in 1996. She then went on to become the first American woman since Peggy Fleming to win three World Figure Skating Championships (or Worlds). She added a fourth in 2001.

Michelle Kwan performs an elegant spin during the 1998 Olympic games.

On figure skating's brightest stage, however, Kwan has experienced disappointment. Many people expected her to win gold medals in the Winter Olympics. She won the silver medal in the 1998 Olympics, then took the bronze medal four years later. Despite her disappointing Olympic finishes, she always remained poised and full of grace.

Although her lifelong goal of winning a gold medal in the Olympics may never be realized, she is a champion. Michelle Kwan will enter the history books as one of the sport's most beloved skaters.

CHAPTER ONE

Family Business

Michelle Wing Kwan was born on July 7, 1980, in Torrance, California. Her parents, Danny and Estella Kwan, had lived in China most of their lives. Danny Kwan grew up in poverty in Canton, and then later in Hong Kong. He wanted his family to have a better life than he had known, so he and Estella Kwan came to the United States in the 1970s after they were married in China. The two of them adapted quickly to Western culture. In fact, Michelle's parents named her after the title of a song by her father's favorite band, The Beatles.

Michelle was the youngest of three children. Her brother Ron was born four years before her, and her sister Karen was born two years after Ron. The Kwans did not have a lot of money. Danny Kwan was part owner of a

Michelle effortlessly leaps through the air during the World Championships in 2002.

Cantonese-style restaurant. He earned just enough from the restaurant to pay the bills. The Kwans were an extremely close family, especially Michelle and Karen. The sisters were best friends. They did almost everything together, including watching television, playing games, and spending time with their grandparents, who lived nearby.

Danny and Estella Kwan encouraged their children to participate in activities outside of school. Michelle and Karen took gymnastics lessons and Ron played hockey at an ice rink near their home in Rancho Palos Verdes, California. Ice hockey was an unusual sport for a boy growing up in southern California, but he loved it. His sisters soon started following him to the rink.

Young Skater

Michelle and Karen were amazed when they saw the hockey players skating up and down the rink. Michelle, who was five at the time, wanted to be out on the ice with her brother. Her parents just laughed and said she was too young. She turned her attention to figure skating when she learned there were lessons given at the rink. She begged her parents to let her and Karen sign up. Again they told her she was too young, but Michelle pleaded until they finally agreed. She was thrilled.

One day a week Michelle and Karen went to the skating rink and took a lesson with a group of children. An instructor first taught them how to fall safely so they would not get hurt when they stumbled or slipped. Then they were taught how to stay on their feet by walking on the ice in their skates. Many of the children grabbed on to the railing. But for Michelle, skating came

Kids play hockey on frozen lake in Maine. Michelle became interested in skating after seeing her brother play the game.

easily. She quickly picked up the basic figure skating techniques, such as **stroking** (pushing outward with the skates to go forward) and **gliding** (moving across the ice using momentum gained from stroking). She was soon skating around the ice easily.

Michelle recalled her earliest days on the ice, saying, "All of us [beginners] had wobbly ankles at first, especially Karen, who's always had long flamingo legs. We wore rented brown skates that were ugly and stiff and hurt our feet, but we didn't care because we were having so much fun skating."[1]

Expensive Sport

Though Michelle hated cold temperatures, she loved the sport. After mastering the basics she started doing jumps, **spins** (twirling the body rapidly in tight circles), and **spirals** (gliding across the ice in a curving pattern with one leg held in the air). As soon as she learned one technique, she asked the instructor to show her another.

After about six months of lessons, an observer told Michelle that she and Karen were good enough for private lessons. But these one-on-one sessions were much more expensive than group lessons. With private lessons Danny would have to pay for the extra time on the ice. Both girls would also need skates of their own. Danny added up the costs and decided it was too expensive.

Michelle and Karen tried to convince their father to change his mind. So did others who had seen Michelle and Karen skate. After the sisters pleaded with their father, he finally agreed. But first they had to promise to

Michelle Kwan completes a spiral at the U.S. Figure Skating Championships in 1994.

Michelle Kwan showed both style and grace early in her career. Here she makes a difficult jump.

keep up their grades in school and to sometimes work in the restaurant. They also had to agree to quit figure skating if it ever stopped being fun.

Traditional Girl

The Kwans were happy that their daughters had found a hobby they liked. But they made sure the girls balanced skating with other interests. Michelle enjoyed collecting stuffed animals, playing basketball, listening to music, and swimming. She also earned good grades in school.

Mr. and Mrs. Kwan also made it a point to teach Michelle, Karen, and Ron the traditions of their Chinese

Michelle Kwan shows her lucky necklace to a crowd at a press conference. The necklace was a gift from her grandmother.

heritage. They especially wanted their children to understand the importance of family. "We speak a mixture of Chinese and English at home," Michelle said. "My father tells lots of stories about the old life in China. I always—even when I skate—wear a necklace that my grandmother gave me. It has a little Chinese dragon on it and a symbol that means good luck. Karen, Ron, and I are very close to our grandparents. Even though they don't speak much English, we understand one another."[2]

Although the family remained important to Michelle and Karen, skating took up more of their time as they advanced in the sport. With the private lessons, the girls were at the rink almost every day. All the practice paid off when Michelle won her first competition at age seven. Karen was also a good skater and won events, too. But the girls' instructor sensed something special in Michelle, even at that early age.

A Bold Leap

Michelle first started to dream about becoming a figure-skating champion while watching the 1988 Winter Olympics on television. When Brian Boitano of the United States won the gold medal in the men's figure skating competition, Michelle told her parents that she wanted to skate in the Olympics someday.

But the Olympics were a long way off for a seven-year-old girl who was still moving up through the **United States Figure Skating Association**'s (USFSA) eight levels: pre-preliminary, preliminary, pre-juvenile, juvenile, intermediate, novice, junior, and senior lady. To advance to a higher level, Michelle had to take an on-ice test showing she had mastered certain skills. When she completed a triple jump (twisted her body around three times in the air and landed on one foot), she reached the junior level at age eleven.

A figure skating pair performs at the 1998 Olympic games. After watching the 1988 Olympics, Michelle decided that she wanted to become a skating champion.

Junior competitions consist of **compulsory figures** (the tracing of figure eights on the ice), a **short program** (a technical program that is two minutes, thirty seconds long), and a **free skate** (a four-minute program designed to show a skater's artistic and technical skills). Michelle loved everything about skating in the junior level except the compulsories. They were highly technical and the judges watched closely for mistakes. The slightest misstep could cost a skater the competition. She was eager to reach the senior lady level, because compulsories were not required at that level.

Although Michelle did not like the compulsories, she practiced them anyway. She and Karen woke up at 4:30 A.M. and skated before school every morning to work on all their techniques. They slept in their skating clothes so they could get ready faster and have more time at the rink.

Gliding across the ice, Michelle goes through her short program at the U.S. Figure Skating Championships in 1997.

After practice one day, the instructor told Danny Kwan that Michelle and Karen had learned all they could at the neighborhood rink. It was time to take them to an official training center, where they could continue to develop their skills. Mr. and Mrs. Kwan again had a difficult decision to make.

Family Sacrifices

A professional instructor would cost more money than the family could afford. Danny already worked a second job to help pay for the girls' skating, and it was barely enough. The girls went nine months without lessons, although they continued to practice at the rink.

Danny knew the family's lack of money was keeping the girls from becoming great skaters. So after careful thought, he and his wife sold their house to pay for instruction. Everyone moved in with Mr. Kwan's parents at their home in Torrance. Michelle was thrilled to be training again, but she was also thankful for the sacrifices the entire family made for her and Karen.

Before long the family was making weekend trips to Ice Castle, a world-class training center. Ice Castle is located in Lake Arrowhead, California, one hundred miles from Torrance.

After training at Ice Castle, Michelle pulled off a series of stunning feats later that year. As an eleven year old at the junior level with no official coach, she won the gold medal at the Southwest Pacific Regional Championship— one of nine competitions of its kind in the United States. By winning, she qualified for the Pacific Coast Sectional

Championship. Only the elite skaters made it that far. But Michelle proved she belonged when she earned a bronze medal. That meant she automatically qualified for the Junior U.S. Figure Skating Championships, or Nationals. The 1992 Nationals were held in Orlando, Florida, and Michelle was one of only twelve skaters in the United States to make it there.

"I was skating really well," she said, "but it all happened so fast we could hardly believe it. I wasn't ready for a national competition! We hadn't been able to afford a coach for nine months. In those days we didn't have any money at all. Selling the house paid off the bills, but after that there wasn't much left."[3]

The Kwans sacrificed a lot to provide Michelle with the expensive training she needed to develop her talent.

Michelle's father, Danny, talks with her at a skate competition in 2001.

Several wealthy people—including New York Yankees owner George Steinbrenner—stepped in and helped finance Michelle's blossoming career. The money paid for her trip to Nationals and for a personal instructor. Legendary figure-skating coach Frank Carroll agreed to take on Michelle as his student.

Taste of Gold

Although Michelle had only three weeks to prepare for Junior Nationals, she made great improvement under her new coach. She could perform difficult jumps in practice and was ready to prove herself at Nationals. But not having a coach for nine months quickly showed once they started. She skated poorly in her short program and free skate, finishing in ninth place. Even though it was her first national competition, she was heartbroken.

Michelle's mood improved when she learned that she and Karen had been accepted as students at Ice Castle. That meant they could live at the facility and practice on the private rink during the week. Their father lived there with the girls and drove back and forth to work every day. Meanwhile Mrs. Kwan stayed in Torrance with Ron, who was finishing high school.

Michelle trains with a choreographer at the Ice Castle International Training Center in Lake Arrowhead, California.

In her first year at Ice Castle Michelle attended a public school at Lake Arrowhead. After that, though, she studied with private tutors so she could spend even more time during the day on skating. Michelle continued to study hard and make good grades. She had an incentive to do well. If her grades slipped, her father would have pulled her out of skating.

Passing the Test

After just one year of skating at the junior level, Michelle was ready to compete at the senior lady level. This was figure skating's top level and included the nation's best skaters, such as Nancy Kerrigan and Tonya Harding. Michelle told Coach Carroll she wanted to take the test required for the senior lady level, but he strongly disagreed. She was only twelve years old. He wanted her to prepare for—and win—Junior Nationals in 1993.

Coach Carroll soon found out this was not in his new student's plans. "Frank went off to a coaches' conference in Canada for a week," she said. "And I did something that I don't usually do: I ignored the wisdom of someone who was older and wiser than me and I took the Senior test. This is a good example of what I mean when I say I'm impatient. I do have a mind of my own, and at that moment I felt like I knew me and my abilities better than anyone else."[4]

Michelle easily passed the test. Telling her coach was the hard part. Carroll was furious and would not talk to her for several days. Finally he sat her down and explained what it meant to skate at that level. He told her most skaters could complete all the difficult jumps, and

Frank Carroll sits beside Michelle Kwan at a 2001 competition. Carroll and Kwan sometimes disagreed about the course of her career.

the truly great ones were also artistic and elegant on the ice. Michelle had grasped the technical part of skating. Artistry and elegance, though, were lacking in her performances. She promised him she would do whatever he asked of her and vowed to work harder than ever to become a champion. Her personal motto became "Work hard, be yourself, and have fun."[5]

A Star on Ice

At age thirteen Kwan began to develop under Coach Carroll's careful instruction. He guided her on the elements that judges watch most closely. One of the first techniques she practiced was her **footwork**, a connecting series of rapid steps that takes a skater across the ice. She also worked hard on becoming more artistic. Her body movements started to flow and match the rhythm of the music.

Physical development also played a part in making Kwan a better skater. She hit a growth spurt and added height and weight, which made her faster and stronger on the ice. Using her new build as well as what she had learned from Carroll, Kwan won both the Senior Regionals and Sectionals in 1993. In her first season at the senior lady level, she qualified for Nationals in Phoenix, Arizona.

Once she got to Nationals, Kwan seemed awestruck by the older skaters. In the free skate she missed some of her jumps and the judges penalized her. She finished in sixth place. Although this was good for a thirteen year old at the senior lady level, it was not good enough for a coach and student who both wanted perfection.

Skating Controversy

After Nationals Kwan won the gold medal at the Gardena Spring Trophy in Italy, her first international

Always striving for perfection, Kwan moves gracefully during her free skate routine at Nassau Coliseum in Uniondale, New York.

competition. She returned to the United States to compete in the Olympic Festival, held in San Antonio, Texas. With twenty-five thousand people watching, Kwan skated beautifully and captured the gold medal. It was one of her proudest moments on the ice.

In 1994 Kwan made it to Nationals in Detroit, Michigan, by again winning Sectionals. Because it was an Olympic year, the silver and gold medalists from Nationals would skate in Norway at the Winter Games. But before the competition started, a man assaulted Nancy Kerrigan, striking her on the knee with a metal rod. Kerrigan had been favored to win. Now that she was out of the event, Kwan had a good chance of finishing first or second. She did not perform at her best, yet she skated well enough to finish second behind Harding. Her dream finally came true. She was headed to the Olympics, and her coach and family could not have been more proud.

Michelle celebrates a silver-medal performance at the 1994 Nationals in Detroit.

The incident at Nationals dominated the news, and Kwan was caught in the middle. The USFSA held a special meeting and decided to send Kerrigan to the Winter Olympics after all. Their decision knocked Kwan out of the Winter Games. Though disappointed, she showed maturity beyond her years when she told reporters that Kerrigan deserved to go. But rumors surfaced that Harding was involved in the assault on Kerrigan. The USFSA sent Kwan to the Olympics as an alternate, just in case Harding was banned from competition. In the end, Harding skated while Kwan observed. Kwan told herself there would be other Olympics.

America's Sweetheart

After the Olympics, Kwan found herself alone in the U.S. skating spotlight. Kerrigan took some time away from competition after winning the silver medal in the 1994 Olympics, then later retired from amateur skating. Harding was banned from skating by the USFSA for her involvement in the Kerrigan assault.

Kwan was the nation's lone representative at the 1994 Worlds in Chiba, Japan. She had trouble with her triple **Lutz jump** (a jump in which a skater takes off from one foot, does the specified number of turns in midair, and lands on the other foot) in the short program. As a result, she was in eleventh place heading into the free skate. Because she was the only U.S. skater in the competition, she had to finish in the top ten to secure two positions for the team in the World Championships the next year. The pressure was on.

Michelle performs a layback spin during the World Championships in 1994. The competition led to a world tour with professional skaters.

Kwan rose to the challenge in the free skate and completed two clean triple Lutzes. The crowd loved her performance. She had moved up three spots to finish eighth.

After Kwan's impressive free skate at Worlds, her popularity in the United States soared. She was invited to join Campbell's Soups Tour of World Figure Skating Champions, which included past champions Brian Boitano, Nancy Kerrigan, and other legends in the sport. "This was a big honor and a chance for me to make some money, which we badly needed. It was also a lot of fun. My mom came with me. After all those years when we were too busy to spend more than five minutes at a time together, it felt so good to sit around our hotel room and tell each other stories. Having her all to myself seemed like a huge luxury."[6]

In 1995 Lori Nichol, a skating teacher from Toronto, Canada, was hired to work on Kwan's **choreography**. Coach Carroll wanted Nichol to create a program that would allow Kwan to skate with more energy and artistry. Kwan's presentation improved, but her technical performance at the 1995 Nationals was not up to her usual high standards. She fell while attempting a triple Lutz in the free skate and finished with the silver medal.

Time to Sparkle

In the months leading up to Worlds in Birmingham, England, Coach Carroll made Kwan's program even harder by including seven triples. She responded to the challenge and skated flawlessly at Worlds. Yet after the short program, she was in fifth place. Before Kwan started her free skate, Coach Carroll said just one word to her: sparkle. That is precisely what she did as she made all the jumps. She even added a double **toe-loop** jump to one of her triples, a difficult **combination**. The crowd loved it, but the judges were not as impressed. They gave her marks that moved her up just one place to fourth. She was hurt and confused by her scores and wondered what went wrong.

After a disappointing performance in the 1995 World Championships, Michelle decided to change her image to reflect her greater maturity.

Carroll told Kwan the judges saw her as a cute little girl instead of a serious and mature skater. Together they decided it was time for her to change that image. Carroll and Nichol choreographed a program around German composer Richard Strauss's musical drama *Salome*. The program allowed Kwan to better express herself. They also changed her image by using makeup and replacing her ponytail with a more mature hairstyle.

When the 1996 season started Kwan put it all together in competition—the jumps, the footwork, the artistry, and the maturity. After skating to *Salome* at Nationals in San Jose, California, the judges awarded her with the gold medal. Karen Kwan finished in fifth place. The girls' parents were extremely proud to have two of the top five skaters in the nation.

Michelle Kwan was confident she could skate at an even higher level. She was in first place after the short program at Worlds in Edmonton, Canada. She then stunned the international audience in the free skate. Instead of finishing with a double **axel** (when a skater takes off from one foot going forward, turns the specified number of times in midair, and lands on the other foot going backward), she completed a triple toe-loop jump. Kwan received two perfect scores and won the gold medal. She became the third-youngest world champion in history.

Chapter Four

Golden Opportunity

After winning Worlds in 1996, Kwan was at the top of her sport, both on and off the ice. Requests to do interviews or photo shoots came nearly every day. She received letters and stuffed animals from children. She returned the favor when she became a national spokesperson for Children's Miracle Network and other charities that benefit kids.

With the 1998 Nationals and the Winter Olympics approaching, Kwan focused entirely on skating. While training for Nationals, she developed pain in her left foot. X rays revealed a slight fracture, which kept her off her feet for three weeks. Coach Carroll altered her program so she would not have to push off from her bad foot during jumps. With her foot still hurting, Kwan gave the performance of a lifetime at the 1998 Nationals. In the free skate she received eight out of nine perfect scores for presentation to win the gold medal.

In the days leading up to the Olympics in Nagano, Japan, Kwan's foot was still sore, so she stayed in California an extra week to treat the injury. Once she got to Japan she stayed outside of Nagano in a hotel with her family, while most of the U.S. athletes stayed in the

Michelle (left), Tara Lipinski (center), and Lu Chen smile with pride after receiving their medals at the 1998 Olympics.

Michelle Kwan's Winning Record

YEAR	PLACE
Nationals	
2002	First
2001	First
2000	First
1999	First
1998	First
1997	Second
1996	First
1995	Second
1994	Second
1993	Sixth
World Championships	
2002	Second
2001	First
2000	First
1999	Second
1998	First
1997	Second
1996	First
1995	Fourth
1994	Eighth
Olympics	
2002	Third
1998	Second

Source: U.S. Figure Skating Association

Olympic Village. Her coach did not want her to get distracted from her goal.

Kwan was in first place after the short program. But her U.S. teammate and rival Tara Lipinski was close behind. Kwan skated before Lipinski in the free skate and gave a clean, but reserved, performance. Kwan knew she had left room for Lipinski to move ahead. Lipinski skated wonderfully and won the gold medal. Kwan won the silver medal.

Kwan later spoke about finishing second. "I was on the podium and I [thought] . . . I wish I was standing a little taller. I wish I was on that first step. But just to hear the anthem, I think it was an honor because it was for the country."[7]

Back on Top

After years of practicing for an Olympic gold medal, Kwan wondered why she had not skated her best. Although she displayed grace when she talked about it to the media, inside she was heartbroken. She wondered if her love for the sport had started to fade. "My father always told me that my love for skating has to come from me and only me. He says if I stop feeling that passion I should stop skating. So I'm always asking myself whether I'm truly happy doing what I'm doing, whether it's truly what I want."[8]

Kwan became more popular after finishing second. Fans were impressed with the way she conducted herself after losing the gold. She received fan mail every day, most of which offered words of encouragement. Before long she was looking at the Olympic experience not as *losing* the gold medal, but as *winning* the silver medal.

A few months later at Worlds in Minneapolis, Minnesota, the crowd cheered wildly for Kwan when she was introduced. She skated with energy and passion. The performance earned her the gold medal for the second year in a row. For the next several years she competed at the same high level. She won Nationals again from 1999 through 2001, and Worlds in 2000 and 2001.

Lost Years

Because Kwan had devoted her teenage years to figure skating, she missed out on the high school experience. In fact, she had not attended school full time since she was in seventh grade—her first year at Ice Castle. When Kwan earned her high school degree, she decided to make up for lost time. She started at UCLA in the fall of 1999.

Although skating had earned the family millions of dollars Kwan had always planned to get a college degree. The Kwans placed a lot of importance on education. So she lived in a dormitory, ate in the cafeteria, and made friends with nonskaters. It was all a big change for someone who had skated nearly every day of her life for the last thirteen years.

Kwan loved school, but she started to feel the effects of not practicing as often as she once did. In one competition she fell during a triple toe-loop—a relatively easy jump. Because 2002 was an Olympic year, she decided to cut back her class schedule and focus mainly on

Michelle (right) completes the beautiful routine that led to a gold medal at the U.S. Figure Skating Championships in 2001.

skating. It was most likely going to be her last chance for an Olympic gold medal.

True Champion

A few months before the 2002 Olympics in Salt Lake City, Utah, Kwan stunned the skating world when she fired her longtime coach. She felt she had learned all she could from Carroll. People openly questioned her decision to make such a drastic change so close to the Winter Games.

Michelle Kwan carries the Olympic flame in 2002.

This time Kwan stayed in the Olympic Village, where she mingled with the other athletes. Once the competition started, she repeated her Olympic success in the short program and moved into first place. Two nights later in the free skate, she fell while attempting a triple jump. The audience was stunned, and so was Kwan. They cheered her on and she recovered to skate well, but it was not enough. When her program ended she left the ice in tears and hugged her father. It was a difficult and emotional moment for two people who had worked so hard and sacrificed so much.

Kwan's disappointing performance dropped her from first place to third. Her U.S. teammate, Sarah Hughes, jumped from fourth place into first. Again, on the medal podium, Kwan handled a painful experience with dignity and grace.

"This Is Why I Love Skating"

Although Kwan has not ruled out another attempt to capture an Olympic gold medal, she will be twenty-five years old during the next Winter Games. That is an age skating experts consider too old to perform at the sport's highest level. For now, though, her love of figure skating remains strong. It keeps her going back to the practice rink. "There [are] so many things that I love about skating," she said. "The audience, the ice, the lights, the music. And when you feel the wind blowing in your face and you feel the chill of the ice and you're just out there, that is when I understand. This is why I love skating."[9]

Notes

Chapter One: Family Business

1. Michelle Kwan, *Heart of a Champion*. New York: Scholastic, 1997, p. 15.
2. Kwan, *Heart of a Champion*, p. 11.

Chapter Two: A Bold Leap

3. Kwan, *Heart of a Champion*, p. 35.
4. Kwan, *Heart of a Champion*, p. 48.
5. Kwan, *Heart of a Champion*, p. 22.

Chapter Three: A Star on Ice

6. Kwan, *Heart of a Champion*, p. 74.

Chapter Four: Golden Opportunity

7. Quoted in NBC, *Today Show*, February 8, 2001.
8. Kwan, *Heart of a Champion*, p. 127.
9. Quoted in NBC, *Today Show*.

Glossary

axel: A jump in which a skater takes off from one foot going forward, spins at least one and a half times in midair, and lands on the other foot going backward.

choreography: The arrangement of music, artistry, and skating in a skater's program.

combination: Two jumps in succession.

compulsory figures: A set of figure eights that skaters carve on the ice; also called school figures. It is the origin of the term "figure skating."

footwork: A series of rapid steps that are required in both the short program and the free skate.

free skate: A four-minute program for ladies (four and a half minutes for men and for pairs) that has no required elements but is choreographed to show a skater's artistic and technical skills; also called a long program.

gliding: Moving across the ice using only momentum gained from stroking.

Lutz jump: While gliding backward, a skater takes off from one back outside edge of the skate, spins at least once in midair, and lands on the back outside edge of the other skate.

short program: A two-minute, forty-second program that consists of eight required elements; also called a technical program.

spins: Artistic moves in which a skater twirls around rapidly in one spot on the ice.

spirals: Artistic moves in which a skater glides across the ice with one leg held in the air. Skaters usually do spirals in curving patterns.

stroking: Pushing off with the inside edges of the blades to make a skater move forward.

toe-loop: While gliding backward, a skater uses the toe pick to launch in the air off the back outside edge of the skate, spins at least once, and lands on the same back outside edge.

United States Figure Skating Assocciation: An organization created in the 1920s to set standards for amateur skating.

For Further Exploration

Books

Michelle Kwan, *Heart of a Champion*. New York: Scholastic, 1997. Kwan writes about her family, her career, and her rise as one of figure skating's greatest champions.

Pohla Smith, *Superstars of Women's Figure Skating*. New York: Chelsea House, 1997. Examines the careers of past figure-skating champions, including Peggy Fleming, Dorothy Hamill, Katarina Witt, and others.

U.S. Figure Skating Association, *The Official Book of Figure Skating*. New York: Simon & Schuster, 1998. Produced by the U.S. Figure Skating Association, this volume is filled with photos and is an excellent reference guide to men's, women's, and pairs' figure skating. Explains skating techniques, competitions, scoring, and more.

Barry Wilner, *Michelle Kwan: Star Figure Skater*. Berkeley Heights, NJ: Enslow, 2001. A biography detailing Michelle Kwan's earliest days on ice skates to the successes and failures she experienced in competition. Provides career statistics.

Websites

The Michelle Kwan Fan Page (http://heatherw.com). Includes the latest news on Kwan, plus her competitive record, personal information, and more.

Skating—Michelle Kwan—Bio (http://sports.espn.go.com). A great source for Kwan's career accomplishments and her records in competition.

Index

Picture
Credits

Cover photo: Associated Press, AP

Associated Press, AP, 11, 12, 13, 16, 17, 21, 25, 26, 28

Associated Press, Coca Cola, 38

Associated Press, CP, 20

© Duomo/CORBIS, 30, 37

© Ferrell Grehan/CORBIS, 9

Chris Jouan, 34

© Wally McNamee/CORBIS, 5, 19, 33

© Reuters NewMedia Inc./CORBIS, 8, 23

About the Author

Raymond H. Miller is the author of more than fifty non-fiction books for children. He has written on a range of topics from sports trivia to stamp collecting. He enjoys playing sports and spending time outdoors with his wife and two daughters.